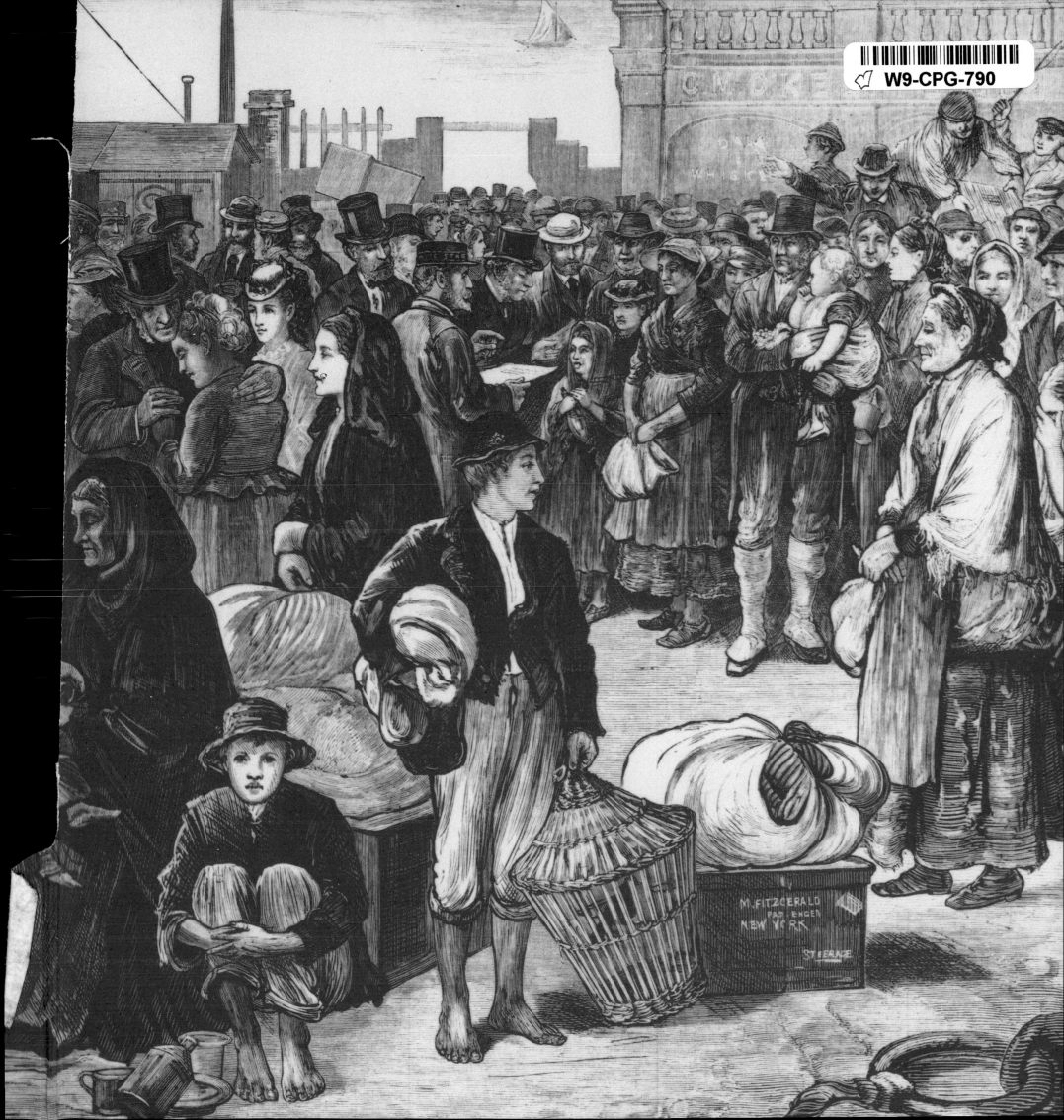

Designed by Philip Clucas
Edited by David Gibbon
Commissioning Editor: Andrew Preston
Photographic Research: Leora Kahn and
Meredith Greenfield

MALLARD PRESS

An imprint of BDD Promotional Books Company, Inc.,
666 Fifth Avenue, New York, NY 10103

Mallard Press and its accompanying design and logo
are trademarks of BDD Promotional Book Company, Inc.

CLB 2733
© 1992 Colour Library Books Ltd, Godalming, Surrey, England
First published in the United States of America
in 1992 by The Mallard Press
Printed and bound in Hong Kong
ISBN 0 7924 5563 0

THE IRISH
AMERICANS

Ernest Wood

MALLARD
PRESS

'91, '92.

en Island,

CONTENTS

IRISH SOCIETIES IN America not only helped countrymen find jobs and adjust to American life, they made them feel at home by perpetuating the ways of the old country as well. The Gaelic Society Hurling and Football Team played matches in the early 1890s up and down the central states, from Philadelphia to Troy, N.Y. and Stamford, Connecticut.

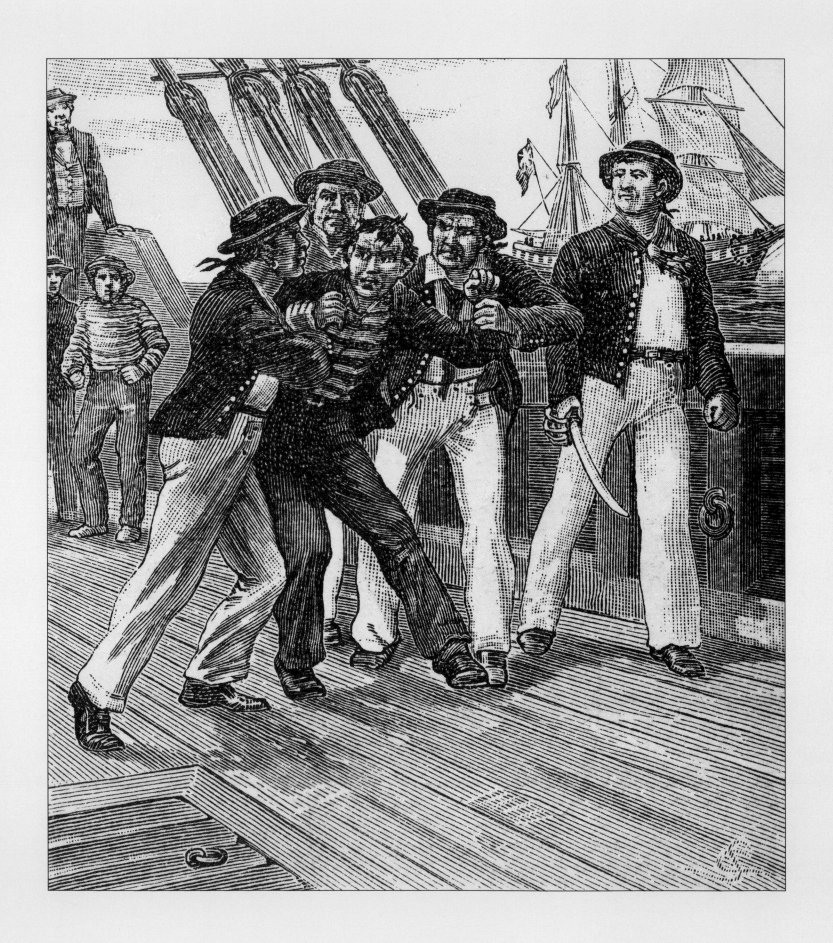

CHAPTER ONE

America's Earliest Irish

THE IRISH CATHOLIC MILLIONS who fled the potato famine of the mid-nineteenth century certainly changed the story of immigrant America. They were the first group to come in a large, sudden wave that was very different in social makeup from the establishment already here. They were not, however, the first Irish to come to America.

IN THE EARLY YEARS, the Irish in America were but a scattered few. As early as 1586, Edward Nugent served in North Carolina with Captain Ralph Lane. The first immigrant group – 140 Northern Irish Presbyterians – set sail from Ulster to New England on the *Eagle Wing* in 1636 – more than 200 years before the famine Irish came over. More than halfway across the Atlantic, the ship met a fierce storm. Convinced the tempest was a sign that their trip was against God's will, the emigrants returned home.

THE IRISH, HOWEVER, HAD looked to the west, and to the future.

IT WAS NOT LONG before Irishmen joined the colonization of the New World. An attempt in the 1650s to found a colony in Maryland called "New Ireland" failed, but by the end of the century the Irish were established in Pennsylvania, Maryland, Delaware and New York. Some Irish did very well for themselves. Thomas Lewis of Belfast, who landed in America in 1656 and became a merchant in Albany, N.Y., was one of the wealthiest men in the colony when he died in 1684. The Colonial Governor of New York at the time was Thomas Dongan, an Irish Catholic from County Kildare.

THE EARLY COLONIES WERE not always so welcoming, however. When Thomas Dongan tried to settle Irish folk on his lands in Massachusetts in about 1710, the local government refused him permission. New England Puritans did not only dislike Catholic Dongan, however, they disliked the Presbyterian Irish too – along with everyone else who did not follow their Puritan creed. In 1692 the people of Salem executed an Irishwoman named Granny Glover as a witch because they thought her native Gaelic was the language of the Devil.

LEFT: EMIGRANTS IN the late 18th and early 19th centuries faced a unique danger – impressment into the British Navy. Above: in 1699, James Logan arrived in Pennsylvania as secretary to William Penn. As mayor of Philadelphia, he authorized the Irish to attend the first public Mass held in the city.

But America was a big country, and there was plenty of room for the Irish. Thousands of miles away another colonial governor played an entirely different role in the Irish colonization of America. Hugh O'Connor, born in Dublin in 1734, fled to Spain to escape troubles with the English and wound up – with his name translated into Spanish as Hugo Oconór – first as a Spanish soldier in New Spain and, from 1767 to 1770, as Governor of Texas.

Irishmen like Hugh O'Connor were fleeing an English domination that had existed since 1169, when King Henry II's knights landed in Ireland. By the 1700s, the most common reasons that emigrants gave for leaving home were mistreatment by landlords, taxes, religious discrimination (against both Protestants and Catholics), and the deteriorating economy. One Irishman wrote that "betwixt landlord and rectors, the very marrow is screwed out of our bones." Foreshadowing events to

Below: Patrick Henry, a Virginian of Irish descent, demonstrated two strong Irish characteristics, the passionate love of freedom and a gift for oratory, when he declared before the Virginia Assembly in 1775, "Give me liberty or give me death!" Right: the Irish filled the rank and file as well as the leadership of the American Revolution. Irishman Patrick Carr was one victim of the Boston Massacre.

ABOVE: MATHEW CAREY, a radical Dublin newspaper editor, left Ireland for Philadelphia in 1784 to avoid prosecution for criticizing the English government. As a prominent publisher, he continued to champion the causes of freedom in Ireland and of the downtrodden and poor on both sides of the Atlantic. Top right: among the signers of the Declaration of Independence were four native Irishmen and four men born of Irish parents.

come, there were crop failures in 1728-30, 1740 and 1757. On top of all this, Ireland in the eighteenth century faced a tremendous population explosion – from a little more than two million Irish people in 1700 to over eight million in 1841. Meanwhile, the Industrial Revolution, which could have given employment to many of these people, passed the island by.

THE RATE OF EMIGRATION to America was at first just a trickle. From North Carolina to upstate New York there had been a few organized Irish settlements before the American Revolution. But most were relatively small. William Johnson, an Indian agent born in Ireland, settled sixty Irish families in Warrenbush, N.Y. in 1740, for example. But the first U.S. Census in 1790 counted only 44,000 people who had been born in Ireland and 150,000 more of Irish ancestry in a total American population of three million. Catholics constituted only a small fraction of the Irish immigrants – the Church estimated it had about 35,000 faithful in the United States.

NO ONE CAN SAY the Irish were not a visible and vital part of the Colonies and the young Republic, however. St. Patrick's Day was celebrated in Boston as early as 1737, and General George Washington recognized it as an official holiday for his Colonial troops. On the eve of the Revolution, an Irishman named Patrick Carr was one of the five persons killed in the Boston Massacre. Three Irishmen pulled down the statue of King George III in New York's Bowling Green and had it melted down for bullets. And Daniel Junior, born in Maryland of Irish ancestry, is credited with coining the phrase: "No Taxation Without Representation." The Irish even accounted for eight signatories of the Declaration of Independence – four of them born in

Left: Charles Carroll, whose grandfather came to America in 1688, was the only Catholic to sign the Declaration of Independence. The Carroll family had been among the aristocracy in Ireland; Carroll was the wealthiest of the declaration's signers. Right: Robert Fulton, an American inventor of Irish descent, developed the first commercially practical steamboat in 1807. By mid-century steam would speed the transatlantic trip for millions of Irish, cutting a voyage that often took eight weeks under sail to just two.

Known as "Father of the American Navy," John Barry, a native of Ireland, was the first American naval commander to capture a British warship during the Revolution. Later, Barry became the first commander of the United States Navy.

Ireland. However, Irishman Charles Carroll III of Maryland was the only Catholic to sign. On July 8, 1776, John Nixon, whose parents had emigrated from County Wexford in the 1680s, was the first to read the document aloud in public. Later, Irishman Thomas Fitzsimons was the only Catholic to sign the U.S. Constitution.

DURING THE REVOLUTION SOME thirty-eight percent of the American forces were Irish. The British Army was heavily Irish as well. But as much as each side relied on their own, they hated the other's Irish. Wrote a British officer of the Americans: "The rebels are chiefly composed of Irish redemptioners and convicts, the most audacious rascals existing." And an American said: "The British regiments [are] composed of the most debauched weavers prentices, the scum of the Irish Roman Catholics who desert upon every occasion."

Passengers by the Bark Edward from Newry.

James Thompson, wife & family

John Moore

George Young

James Young

John Henry

Catherine Henry

William Robinson

Isabella Robinson

John Boyd

Henry Hutchinson

R. M'Clatchey

Wm. M'Kibbin

Patrick Doran

Thomas Cox

Nancy Cox

Wm. Annit

James Parker

Hugh Mackey

Edward Lappin

Chas. Holland

Felix M'Groeggan

Pat. Byrne

James M'Nally

Nancy M'Nally

Eliza M'Nally

Alex. Lewis

John Tumelty

Robert Keth, wife and family

John Shannon

John Thompson wife & family

Richard Cox

Marg Bailey

Joseph Orr

Agnes Orr

James Scott

Henry Daries

James Sloane

Felix Cull

Wm Scott

John Mulhollan

Wm. Ruddock

Stewart Cooper

Betty Cooper

James M'Lory

Patrick Magee

Mary Magee

Margaret Magee

John Lewis, wife and family

Owen Small

Kitty Small

Wm. Sloan

LEFT: THE PASSENGER list of the bark Edward, *sailing for America in 1812, included only four families; the rest were either single people or childless couples. In contrast to other European groups, who came as families or sent the father ahead to earn passage for his wife and children, most Irish immigrants were young. When they sent passage money home, they most often brought over unmarried brothers or sisters. Below: John C. Calhoun, vice president under Andrew Jackson, who split with the president over the issue of states' rights, was as proud of his Irish ancestry as he was of his South Carolina home.*

ABOVE: GRANDSON OF an Irish immigrant who landed on Cape Cod in 1729, Dewitt Clinton was instrumental, as Governor of New York, in the founding of a statewide public school system, and oversaw the completion of the Erie Canal, which employed thousands of Irish in its construction. Above right: Andrew Jackson, whose parents emigrated from Ireland, received important support from the American Irish in the 1828 election. They considered him a hero for defeating the British in the War of 1812, and embraced the Jacksonian Democrats for their support of the common man and opposition to the anti-Catholic nativist movement.

NO MATTER WHAT AMERICA thought of them, however, the Irish were enthusiastic about America – and willing to do most anything to get here. Many who could not afford the passage came to be sold upon arrival as indentured servants along with the merchandise that the ship brought. In 1734, the *Charleston Gazette* advertised "Irish servants, men and women, of good trades, from the north of Ireland, Irish linen, household furniture, butter, cheese, chinaware and all sorts of dry goods." By the 1770s there were not enough ships to carry all the people who wished to leave Ireland.

ONE THEY SET SAIL, emigrants were not free of problems either. For next they faced the British Navy's impressment of seamen and passengers. As early as 1795, the American ship *Cincinnatus*, bound from Belfast to Philadelphia, was boarded off the coast of Newfoundland. One passenger wrote that the English captain "pressed every one of our hands save one and near fifty of my fellow passengers, who were most of them flying to avoid the tyranny of a bad government at home, and who thus most unexpectedly fell under the severest tyranny … which exists." In the summer of 1811, the British sloop *Atalanta* stopped and boarded the *Belisarius*, one of thirteen ships intercepted in the year before the War of 1812 broke out. One sailor is said to have told the unfortunate passengers: "We shall suffer no more emigration to that damned Democratic country."

CHAPTER TWO

The Irish Arrive

DEPENDING ON THE WEATHER, the trip from Ireland to America on a sailing ship usually took between four and eight weeks, with an extra two weeks for Southern ports such as Charleston or Savannah. Emigrants were offered few choices in destination because the ships they traveled in were not really fitted out for passengers. They were freight carriers heading for America to pick up goods to be sold in Europe. Most traveled to New York and Philadelphia. The Irish were human ballast for the westward voyage. If the ship had not stocked enough provisions for a voyage unexpectedly extended by uncooperative winds or bad weather, conditions on board could be severe – nearly all ships suffered from overcrowding. Traveling in steerage below decks, passengers were usually separated by sex, with married couples between them. Berths were shared, and the air, which quickly became foul when hundreds of people lived, ate, became ill, gave birth and died together in close quarters, was sometimes fumigated with vinegar.

LATER, STEAMSHIPS MADE THE voyage quicker – about two weeks – and easier. Prophetically, the first steamer to cross the Atlantic from east to west, in 1837, was Irish – the *Sirius* out of Cork. Steam travel did not take over immediately, however. As late as 1856, only five percent of immigrants were traveling by steamer. The same slow, crowded conditions that the Irish had endured in sailing ships for more than a hundred years prevailed. But when steam travel developed in earnest, the switch from sail was quick. By 1863, forty-five percent of emigrants were traveling by steamships. In 1866, the number had grown to eighty-one percent, and by 1870 hardly any traveled by sail any more.

BY THE EARLY- TO mid-nineteenth century, conditions for the rural Irish in Ireland had deteriorated rapidly as landlords increased rents and subdivided farms. One farm, which had had a single tenant in 1793, had ninety-six in 1847. In 1824, forty families – about 200 individuals – who could not pay their rent were displaced from a single farm and were reduced to begging on the highway.

PARTIALLY AS A RESULT of shrinking farms, the rural Irish became almost totally

POLITICAL CARTOONISTS ON both sides of the Atlantic were quick to note that English aid to the Irish was insufficient during the potato famine. In fact, more aid came from America. Frank Leslie's Illustrated Newspaper *(left) of 1880 showed "Columbia keeping the wolf, famine, from the Irish cabin-door." The English magazine* Punch *(above) depicted John Bull giving alms to the poor in 1846.*

dependant for food on the potato – which would feed nearly three times the number of people as wheat from the same amount of land. But then disaster struck. A potato crop failure in the 1820s spurred some emigration from the island. But the massive potato famine of the 1840s turned Ireland into a nation of emigrants.

OFF AND ON FOR years there had been partial failures of the potato crop. Whenever the weather was damp and cold, potato fungus grew rapidly, turning leaves brown and the tubers soft and purple. In July 1845 heavy rains started, and by August the potato blight had appeared. But that summer was only a prelude to the worst.

IN 1846, AGAIN IN July, the same blight struck – with a quickness and harshness not seen before. A priest on a trip to Dublin wrote that he saw luxuriant crops turn to "one wild waste of putrefying vegetation" within a week. "In many places," he wrote, "the wretched people were seated on the fences of their decaying gardens, wringing their hands, and wailing bitterly at the destruction that had left them foodless."

EMIGRATION WAS THE only hope for many starving Irish farmers. In 1851, this family received the blessing of the parish priest before making the voyage to America.

Left: Irish farms supported so many tenants that when one was evicted, these neighbors dug his potato crop to feed themselves. Already poor, the rural Irish were driven to starvation when the potato blight struck in the mid-1840s, devastating their principal source of food.

So the Irish began to leave their homes – in huge numbers.

Since 1830, when emigration to America topped 20,000 for the first time, the numbers leaving Ireland had been steadily increasing. A year before the blight, 75,000 Irish emigrated, two thirds of whom came to the United States. However, by 1847, when the effects of the blight had become undeniable, these numbers had doubled. The following year, most Irish emigrants turned *en masse* towards America. The numbers continued rising steadily until 1851, when 219,000 Irish left for the United States. In all, the famine years accounted for as many as 1.5 million deaths and sent more than a million Irish to America.

That was just the beginning. Though no single year reached the numbers for 1851, and none topped 100,000 after 1854, the Irish still came in a steady stream that only began to slow towards the end of the century. The attractions of America and the distress in Ireland were so strong that not even the American Civil War could stop emigration. In both 1863 and 1864, with another famine at home, 94,000 Irish

though Ellis Island is best known as New York's immigrant entry point, more Irish actually entered via its predecessor, Castle Garden. Once a site for circuses and concerts, Castle Garden was made the point of entry in 1855, and by the time Ellis Island was opened in 1892, Irish immigration had peaked.

emigrated there. An Irish newspaper *The Freeman's Journal*, wrote that "the battlefield has not so much terrors for the Irish tenant farmers as has the struggle for life … at home." In all, some four million Irish came to America between 1845 and the turn of the century – a third of them between 1847 and 1854. The Irish were never the largest immigrant group in America, but they accounted for a far greater percentage of their home population – half of Ireland's eight million people – than any other nation. No other country lost more than a fifth of their population in emigration.

THE REASONS FOR CHOOSING America were simple. Many Irish spurned British colonies because of their centuries-old hatred of the English. Besides, though passage to Canada cost slightly less than to the United States, the fare to Australia was four times greater. The most compelling reason for coming to the United States, however, was the country's reputation as the land of opportunity. Letters home from Irish already in America seductively testified to its opportunities. In 1850 a young woman in New York wrote to her father, saying that "any man or woman without a family are fools that would not venture and come to this plentiful Country where no man or woman ever hungered or ever will and where you will not be seen naked." Twenty years later, a farmer in Iowa wrote to his brother: "An unmarried man or girl can make out a living in any part of the country and have money too, provided he is not afraid to work."

OF COURSE, THE IRISH already in America sent home more than letters. They sent money.

AT CASTLE GARDEN, tired and bewildered immigrants like those in this 1880 woodcut could buy railroad tickets, exchange money and get advice and assistance from public officials. Transfer barges ferried immigrants from Castle Garden to the Erie Railway and a new life.

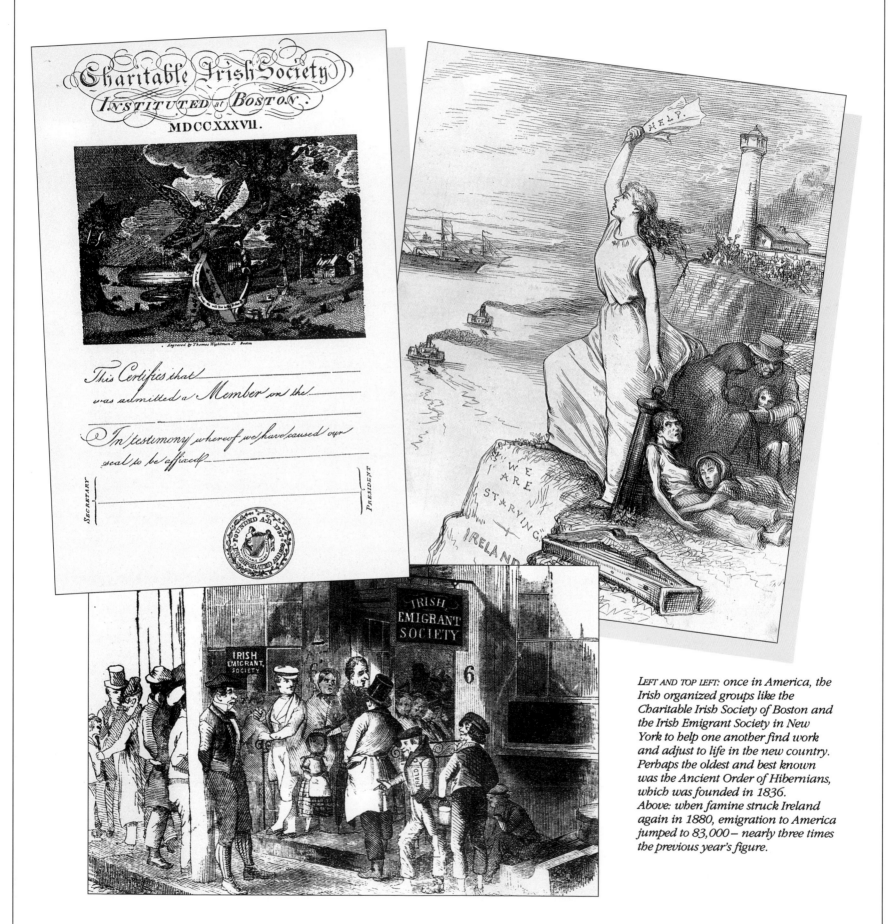

LEFT AND TOP LEFT: *once in America, the Irish organized groups like the Charitable Irish Society of Boston and the Irish Emigrant Society in New York to help one another find work and adjust to life in the new country. Perhaps the oldest and best known was the Ancient Order of Hibernians, which was founded in 1836.*
Above: *when famine struck Ireland again in 1880, emigration to America jumped to 83,000 — nearly three times the previous year's figure.*

THIS CARTOON FROM 1854 is titled "Homeward Bound," but with conditions in Ireland still grim, fewer Irish returned home than other Europeans. Instead, most praised the freedom and opportunities for work in America and urged family and friends to emigrate as well.

BY THE EARLY 1840s, even before the famine, Irish in America were sending home about $1 million a year. When famine struck, the amounts increased dramatically. Several cities established funds to aid famine relief in Ireland. In 1847, Boston sent $50,000; New York $102,000; Philadelphia $55,000 and New Orleans $50,000. Ships also sailed for Ireland with food. It was individual Irish men and women who made the largest contributions, however. Most sent money as they could get it, usually five or ten dollars at a time – though about forty percent of remittances came as prepaid tickets to America. Young women working as domestics sent more than any other group. In 1848, the Irish sent home $2.3 million; in 1849, they sent $4.8 million, and in 1854 they were sending home $8.6 million. As immigrants became settled and took on obligations of their own, contributions decreased. But when famine struck Ireland again in the 1880s, American Irish once more gave generously. In all, between 1848 and 1887 Irish immigrants sent home more than $170 million.

CHAPTER THREE

The Irish Find a New Home

THE IRISH WHO FLED the famine and those who followed were different from the Irish who migrated to America during the seventeenth, eighteenth and early nineteenth centuries. While the "Famine Irish," as they came to be known, were both Protestant and Catholic, by far the greater number were Catholic. And while the earlier immigrants and those who came during the famine years often traveled as families, those who followed more often than not were single people. They were young – overwhelmingly between fifteen and thirty-five years old. They came in about equal numbers of women and men. And they came to stay. Only about ten percent of the Irish returned home, compared to eighty percent of some immigrant groups.

IN THE EARLIEST YEARS, more Irish settled in Pennsylvania than in any other colony, followed by New York and Maryland. From there, they moved west and traveled down the Shenandoah Valley into Virginia and North Carolina. In South Carolina and Georgia the Irish landed at Charleston or Savannah and spread west from there. Augusta, Georgia, was settled by Irishman William O'Bryan in 1735. Old maps of Georgia show places named Limerick, Clare, Killarney, Tyrone, Blarney, Cork, Belfast, Newry and Donegal. From western Carolina, Virginia and Pennsylvania the Irish pushed west into Tennessee and Kentucky. There, as in the eastern colonies, the Irish were frontier farmers, settling the virgin territory of the new world.

THERE ALWAYS HAD BEEN organized Irish settlements and individuals who brought groups of Irish to America. In the mid-1700s, Boice Cooper settled first in Portsmouth, then in Pemaquid, Maine. He returned to Ireland, where he gathered a group of settlers and brought them back to Maine. In the 1820s and 1830s, impresarios who received grants of land from the Mexican government settled colonies of Irish Catholics in south Texas. One town settled this way was named San Patricio de Hibernia (St. Patrick of Ireland). By 1850, San Patricio and neighboring Refugio counties were more than half Irish – while people of Mexican descent numbered only one sixth of the population. The Irish colonies eventually

TWELVE IRISH-BORN men and fourteen others with Irish surnames died at the Battle of the Alamo during Texas' war for independence from Mexico. From Spanish colonial times to 19th-century Irish colonies, the Irish were fundamental to the settlement of the Lone Star State.

failed, victims of disease, hostile Indians and war with Mexico. But the Irish presence in Texas was established. In 1836, twelve Irish-born men and another fourteen with Irish surnames died defending the Alamo during the Texan war for independence from Mexico.

SETTLEMENT PATTERNS CHANGED WHEN the "Famine Irish" arrived in the mid-nineteenth century. Instead of moving to farms, most settled in cities or followed work on canals and railroads through rural areas until they reached the cities at the other end. When they did live on the frontier, most Irish settled in frontier towns such as Butte, Montana, where there was a thriving copper-mining industry. The gold fields of California also attracted a healthy share of Irish.

INDIVIDUAL IRISH WERE RECORDED in the far west as early as 1800, when "Honest Joe" O'Cain traded otter skins with Aleuts and Russians in the Pacific Northwest. In 1824 an Irishman called Don Timoteo Murphy raised cattle and kept Irish greyhounds on a land grant near San Rafael, California. And, in 1834, an Irishman called Jose O'Donoju arrived with troops at the mission in Los Angeles. And there

LEFT: OSCAR FAGAN on horseback in front of the Peter Fagan ranch house, Refugio, Texas, c1898. Above: members of the Irish community at a gathering following Sunday Mass in the Nueces River bottoms near Gussettville, Texas, c1909.

BELOW: ATTEMPTING TO cross the Rocky Mountains by an untried pass in 1846, the Donner Party was snowbound for months, losing 40 of its 87 members. Irishman Patrick Breen kept a diary that chronicled the horrors the travelers faced in the cold.
Right: thirty-one Irish with the Seventh Cavalry died with General George Armstrong Custer at The Little Big Horn in 1876. In the late 19th century, the Irish were the largest foreign-born group among Cavalry soldiers serving in the West.

were Irish cowboys. An Irishman named Joe McCoy established Abilene, Kansas, as a railhead for cattle drives, and Texas Ranger Lee McNelly earned fame for putting down cattle rustling. The outlaw and gunfighter known as Billy the Kid was born in New York of Irish parents.

IN THE LATE 1840s there were so many Irish fighting with the American troops in the Mexican War that the term "Gringo" is said to have originated with Mexicans who misunderstood the lyrics as the Irish sang the traditional song "Green Grow the Rushes." Later, there were Irishmen in the cavalry units of the West. One officer in Wyoming noted: "I preferred the Irish – they were more intelligent and resourceful as a rule." Thirty-one Irish are numbered among the soldiers killed with General George Armstrong Custer at The Little Big Horn. A number of Irish families were victims of an earlier tragedy when, as members of the Donner Party, they became stranded by blizzards in the Rocky Mountains on their way to California. Forty of the eighty-seven in the party died, and the hardships, horrors, deaths and – eventually – cannibalism that were part of the ordeal were recorded in a journal by survivor Patrick Breen, who had come with his family to America from County Cavan.

However, Irish settlements were spread thinly outside the cities. Between 1899 and 1910, the decade in which Oklahoma gained statehood, for example, only 122 of the 440,000 Irish – one in 3,600 – who entered the United States declared the new state to be his destination. Which is not to say that the ones who did go there had lost their Irishness. Shamrock, Oklahoma, an oil boom town developed between 1912 and 1915 by Edwin L. Dunn, a Tulsa Realtor of Irish ancestry, had a main street named Tipperary Road and others named Dublin, Ireland, Cork and Killarney. Its newspapers were named the *Blarney* and the *Brogue*, and many of its buildings were painted green.

It is ironic that the Irish, who had been a rural people in their own country and who in earlier generations had been farmers in America, should now become city dwellers. Perhaps they avoided frontier life because their culture was essentially a sociable one. In 1821 a homesick farmer in Missouri compared rural life in Ireland to America: "I could then go to a fair, or a wake, or a dance …. I could spend the winter's nights at a neighbor's house cracking jokes by the turf fire … but here everyone can get so much land … that they calls them neighbors that live two or three miles off."

There were other reasons why the Irish stayed in cities. Having left Ireland because of devastating crop failures, many of the "Famine Irish" surely wanted to start over in professions more secure than farming. Besides, the Irish simply were not equipped to farm on the scale required in America. In Ireland, where more and more tenants were squeezed each year onto a limited parcel of land, their farms had been small; in America, farms were much larger – huge in the West. Arriving poor, the Irish often did not have the money to travel to the undeveloped areas where farmland was available. They wanted jobs that paid cash so they could send money home. Also, arriving as single people they did not have the help they needed in an era when most farming was a family enterprise.

As a result, seventy-two percent of Irish-Americans in 1870 lived in the seven states with the largest cities: Massachusetts, Connecticut, New York, Pennsylvania, New Jersey, Ohio and Illinois.

San Francisco, which had become a major urban center during the 1849 Gold Rush, was home to 4,200 first-generation Irish folk in 1852 and more than 30,000 by 1880. By 1900 the Butte, Montana, area held 12,000 Irish people – twenty-five percent – giving it the highest percentage of Irish inhabitants in the country.

There was a simple reason why the Irish and other immigrants flocked to one area over another: jobs. Devastated by the Civil War, the South could offer few jobs to attract immigrants during the late nineteenth century. Meanwhile, unlikely spots like Butte boomed. An observer in Milwaukee noted the Irish willingness to move from city to city in order to find work when he wrote in 1854: "They either remain here or go to some other city not far off or some railroad or canal about to be built

One of the West's most famous outlaws, Billy the Kid was born Henry McCarty on New York's Lower East Side in 1859 and moved to New Mexico with his family when he was 14. The Kid was by no means the only Irishman in New Mexico: his partners included men named O'Keefe, O'Folliard and McCloskey.

THE IRISH STREAMED west with thousands of other fortune hunters in the 1849 California Gold Rush. Most were single (in 1850 women accounted for only 8 percent of the California population — only 2 percent in mining districts), and many came directly from Ireland or from Pacific Rim countries. These men panned for gold in the Dakotas.

in order to get the means to buy in future a home in the West." Only one Irishman in twenty came to Milwaukee directly from their native land, he said.

SAN FRANCISCO PROBABLY EXEMPLIFIES better than any other city how willing the Irish were to relocate in order to find jobs. In 1852, only 5.1 percent had come directly from Ireland, while 44.6 percent had come from New York, Philadelphia, Boston, New Orleans and other cities in the Eastern United States. James Phelan was one. When but a boy he had emigrated to New York, where he worked as a grocery clerk. Then, with the first word of gold in California, he left for San Francisco, where he ran a saloon, invested in real estate and founded a bank. By 1870 he had become one of the city's ten richest men. The American Irish, however, were prepared to relocate from farther afield than New York. In 1852, for example, some 44.5 percent of San Francisco's Irish had first settled in Australia, Hawaii or other Pacific Rim lands. They uprooted themselves once more to seek their fortunes in the California gold fields.

CHAPTER FOUR

The Irish Find Work

COMING FROM THEIR SMALL farms to American cities, the Irish who arrived after the famine mostly took unskilled jobs. The women became domestic servants or worked in mills. The men performed the most difficult, backbreaking and dangerous tasks, such as mining, digging canals or laying railroads. In the pre-Civil War South, they often were given jobs that were too dangerous for valuable slaves. Irish were recruited from Boston, for example, to replace slaves digging the Brunswick Canal in Georgia, where one writer noted, "… if the Paddies are knocked overboard or get their backs broke, nobody loses anything." Crews laying railroad tracks in the mountains around Port Jervis, New York, lowered Irish drillers in wicker baskets from ledges down to the blasting areas. There, the man would drill his hole, plant the charge, light the fuse and – if all went well – be pulled to safety before the charge went off. Railroad building was so hazardous that there was said to be "an Irishman buried under every tie" of the American railroad system.

NONETHELESS, MOST IRISH WERE happy to be in America. Andrew Greenlees wrote to his brother in 1853 that "this is a free country, Jack's as good as his master, if he don't like one then go to another. Plenty of work and plenty of wages, plenty to eat and no landlords, that's enough, what more does a man want?"

Pennsylvania's Chesapeake and Ohio Canal placed recruiting notices in Irish newspapers promising "meat three times a day, plenty of bread and vegetables, with a reasonable allowance of liquor, and eight, ten or twelve dollars a month for wages." As a result of such recruiting, some industries had huge concentrations of Irish workers. By 1900, three of every five miners at the Anaconda Mine in Butte were Irish. Wrote one newspaper, "There are several sorts of power working at the fabric of this Republic – water-power, steam-power, and Irish-power. The last works hardest of all."

WHILE THE MEN HELPED turn the wheels of American transportation and industry, Irish women helped the affluent run their homes. They met some opposition. Advertisements for domestics often requested "Protestant girls," or noted "No Irish

THE MOST POPULAR employment for Irish women was as maids, cooks and other household servants. The domestic pictured below right had the help of modern technology to press linens. Many young Irish women also found employment as seamstresses and laundresses, such as these women pressing silk underwear (right) around the turn of the century.

ABOVE: MARY MALLON, an Irish cook known as "Typhoid Mary," was the first identified typhoid carrier in the United States. In 1915, at age 48, she was incarcerated at a New York hospital, where she remained until her death in 1938.
Left and above left: after domestic service, Northeastern textile mills were the largest source of employment for Irish women. Textile work absorbed so many immigrants after 1815 that in some mills more than half the workers were Irish born.

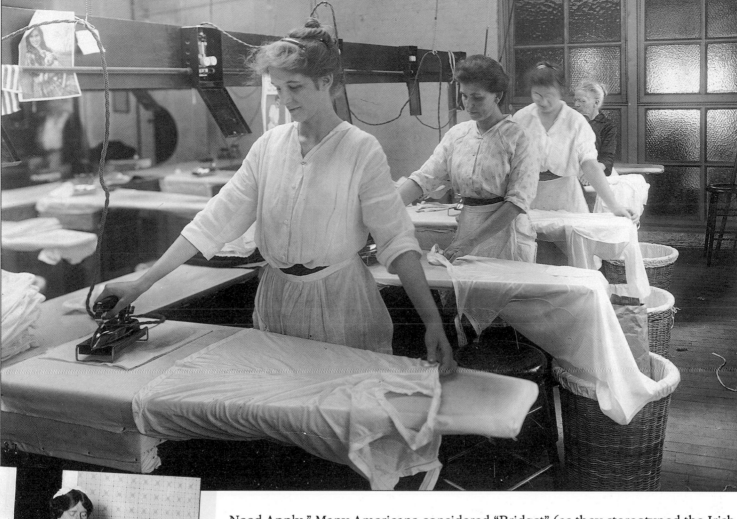

Need Apply." Many Americans considered "Bridget" (as they stereotyped the Irish domestic), clumsy, lazy, an indifferent housekeeper and a poor cook. Irish maids were blamed for broken dishes. They were accused of stealing food. They were docked in pay when they left the house without permission. But because most Americans turned up their noses at domestic work, Irish women had no trouble finding jobs in service. Even the poorest, most naïve girls could find work. In 1851, a New York family is said to have employed a girl who descended stairs backward – because she had used only a ladder in Ireland. More tragic was the case of Mary Mallon, a native of County Tyrone, who became infamous as "Typhoid Mary." The first typhoid carrier recognized in the United States, Mary was the known cause of at least three deaths and fifty-three cases of the disease, many of which occurred while she was employed as a cook by wealthy families living or vacationing in such places as Mamaroneck, Tuxedo Park or Oyster Bay, New York.

IRISH WOMEN SUCCEEDED AS domestics, however, because they arrived single, already spoke English and were willing to work eighty-hour weeks and put up with

ABOVE: IN 1819, an Irishman in South Carolina wrote that "a man who can set up a small store in the country is superior to any other." Shops like this turn-of-the-century New York grocery were even more popular among the urban Irish. Left: a step up from unskilled labor, draying and hauling were popular trades for the Irish in both cities and on the frontier. In Milwaukee in 1850, 40 percent of teamsters, cabmen and carriers were Irish. These teamsters hauled wood in Arizona in the 1870s.
Right: saloonkeeping was a popular trade for the Irish who sought to rise from the unskilled labor pool. As early as 1850, for example, more than 900 of the 1,500 establishments selling liquor in Boston were operated by Irish. Here New Yorkers mourn the beginning of Prohibition with one last drink.

little privacy and constant demands on their time. With room and board and sometimes uniforms provided, the typical Irish maid could send home her share of cash to finance the emigration of others.

IF THEY DID NOT take work as domestics, most immigrant Irish women found work in mills. In 1870, 57.7 percent of the women working in the textile mills in Lowell, Massachusetts, had been born in Ireland.

LIKE THE MEN, MANY women sang the praises of their new life in America. A seamstress in Connecticut wrote home: "I am getting along splendid and likes my work … it seems like a new life. I will soon have a trade and be more independent … you know it was always what I wanted so I have reached my highest ambition."

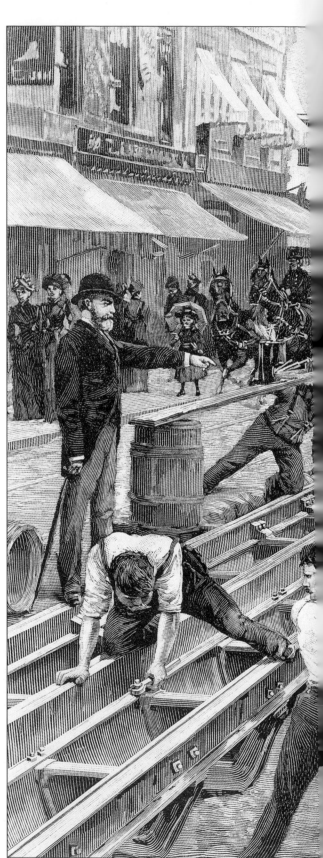

UNSKILLED WHEN THEY arrived in America, many Irishmen went to work as laborers digging canals and tunnels and laying railroads. Both were backbreaking and often dangerous jobs. Large numbers of New York Irish found work, both above and below ground, on construction projects such as the Broadway Surface Railroad (right), and later the Midtown Hudson Tunnel (above).

MANY IRISH REACHED THEIR ambition quickly. Some opened saloons, groceries or shops. Others moved up from common laborers to draymen, carpenters, painters or milkmen. In New York in the 1850s, a third of the shoemakers were Irish and three-quarters of foreign born masons, plasterers and bricklayers were Irish. In Colorado in the 1880s, Irish on the railroad were not only laborers, they were engineers, firemen, brakemen, switchmen, foremen and superintendents.

SOME OF THEIR SUCCESS in finding and keeping such employment was due to the efforts of labor unions. But even when they were not organized, the Irish had a tradition of helping each other find and keep work. In Butte, a member of the territorial legislature complained that "of two men equally competent to fill a position, the Irishman invariably got it." When organized, the Irish became able leaders in many trades, ranging in diversity from millinery and carpet weaving to team driving. They also appeared as members of organizations as diverse as Knights

ABOVE: NAMED FOR a secret society in Ireland, the Molly Maguires conducted a campaign of violence against mine operators in Pennsylvania from the 1850s to the 1870s. Ironically, they were infiltrated by an Irish Pinkerton agent, James McParlan, and prosecuted by another Irishman, Franklin B. Bowan. Following their trial, 20 members of the organization were hanged. Left: subway construction workers, New York 1932.

ABOVE: GEORGE MEANY (left), whose parents were born in Ireland, presided with Walter Reuther over the merger of the American Federation of Labor and the Congress of Industrial Organizations. He later became the most powerful labor leader in America.

MANY LOCAL UNION leaders, such as Michael Quill (facing page top left) of the Transport Workers Union in New York, were Irish. A transport strike headed by Quill in 1948 ended in a matter of hours, however, after another Irishman, New York Mayor William O'Dwyer, appeared before strikers and appealed for an end to the strike. Below: the show of hands in this news photo records the strikers' decision to return to work. Right: born in Ireland, the daughter of a railroad worker and widow of an iron-moulder, Mary Harris Jones, known as "Mother Jones," was an active labor leader into her 90s.

FACING PAGE BOTTOM LEFT: Joe Ryan, leader of the International Longshoremen's Association, whose "goons" are shown (facing page top right) gathered in demonstration at a New York pier during a strike in 1954. Ryan is pictured shaking hands with crime boss Anthony Anastasia.

THE IRISH BEGAN their long association with firefighting in the days of volunteer departments, when fighting a fire also meant fighting rival units to put out the blaze.

of Labor, the American Federation of Labor and the Actors Equity Association. Mary Harris Jones, known as "Mother Jones," an Irish-born member of the Knights of Labor and activist with the United Mine Workers during the late nineteenth and early twentieth centuries, was still speaking at the strike meetings of a West Virginian coal strike when she was ninety-three.

LEFT: AN ENGRAVING of firefighting in the 1870s. Top: the Caldwell Kansas Fire Department in the 1890s. Above: T. Burgett of Galion, Ohio, receives an award from Fire Chief Kenlon.

THOUGH NOT ACTUALLY A labor union, the famous Molly Maguires were a secret society of Irish Pennsylvanian miners who used violence to strike back at unscrupulous and oppressive mine owners. They operated from the 1850s until their capture in the 1870s. Twenty of the Mollies, including leader John Kehoe, were hanged in what is believed to be the largest civilian, non-slave execution up to that time. Ironically, the principal people involved in bringing about the demise of the Molly Maguires were also Irish: Pinkerton detective James McParlan, who infiltrated the organization, had emigrated to Chicago in 1867; Chief Prosecutor Franklin B. Gowan, born in Philadelphia, was the son of Irish immigrants.

BY THE TURN OF THE century, however, seventy-five percent of America's 1.2 million Irish males in blue-collar jobs were classified as skilled labor. Meanwhile, women were filling skilled positions too, as secretaries, clerks, bookkeepers, nurses and teachers. The daughters of Irish immigrants would become the largest ethnic group among teachers.

OF ALL THE PROFESSIONS associated with the Irish, however, the police take the top position. New York had a police marshal named John McManus in 1815. But it was not until the 1840s that most cities established large, modern police forces. The timing could not have been better for the famine Irish, who joined in large numbers, seeking the security of a public-service job and the excitement that police work involved. By the time of the Civil War, New York's police force was twenty-eight percent Irish, despite accounting for only sixteen percent of the city's population. Elsewhere, the Irish filled police forces from Boston to New Orleans to San Francisco. They also had a tradition of serving in volunteer fire departments – whose colorful history included racing other units to fires and brawling with rival fire companies for the privilege of putting out the blaze. Though tamed by city regulations, the Irish continued to serve as firefighters when fire departments, too, became public after the Civil War.

THE FAMINE IRISH arrived just as American cities were creating modern police forces in the 1840s and 1850s, and they joined up in huge numbers. By the late 1880s, the New York Police Department was 28 percent Irish, while the city at large was only 16 percent Irish. Above: an early police raid on illegal gambling. Right: a New York policeman rescues a foundling child.

CHAPTER FIVE

The Irish Become Americans

BEGINNING WITH THE anti-Catholic Know-Nothing campaigns of the 1850s and continuing through such issues as the Civil War draft or election day hooliganism, the Irish often found themselves fighting pitched street battles against Americans – or other Irish. Right: an early woodcut depicts a riot in Philadelphia. Overleaf: riot in Elm Park, New York, between Protestant and Catholic Irish, 1870.

T IS MORE THAN a little ironic that the Irish cared so much for public service in America – because the American public cared so little for the Irish. The animosity was long standing. In 1692 a government official in Maryland wrote that his region was "pestered" by Scotch and Irish immigrants, and in 1729 a Pennsylvanian Quaker named James Logan, himself having immigrated from Ireland thirty years earlier, expressed the fear that "if they continue to come, they will make themselves proprietors of the province." When large numbers of Irish really did arrive after the famine, an eminent Bostonian showed little interest in welcoming them. "Our Celtic fellow citizens," he wrote, "are almost as remote from us in temperament and constitution as the Chinese." In the popular stereotype, Irish women, especially those employed as domestics, were foolish and careless, and Irish men were drunken, dirty, violent and lazy. By the 1850s, many early Presbyterian Irish immigrants began calling themselves "Scotch-Irish" to set themselves apart from the new arrivals.

MORE SERIOUS WAS ANTI-IRISH violence. In Massachusetts alone, houses were stoned (Boston, 1829), Yankee laborers rioted against Catholics employed on construction jobs (Lowell, 1831), and a convent was burned (Charlestown, 1834) – all this before the famine immigrants arrived. Philadelphia had to declare martial law to stop anti-Catholic and anti-Irish riots in 1844. By the 1850s, the Know-Nothing Party – the leading edge of the Nativist movement that advocated "America for Americans" – was marshaling both public opinion and physical violence against the Irish. Riots broke out in Philadelphia, Newark, Baltimore, Brooklyn, St. Louis and several Massachusetts cities. In Louisville, Know-Nothings rioted against both Germans and Irish, setting fires and looting stores and houses until many of the immigrants fled the city. A popular jingle in San Francisco in 1854 declared:

The Know-Nothings have done the job   Just say you're a mick
Wide-awake boys acted accordin'   And they'll kick you on the
If you want to get a lick   other side of Jordan.

ONE OF THE NATIVISTS' fears was that the Catholic Irish would give their allegiance to Rome instead of America. But with the outbreak of The Civil War, a test of the Irish immigrants' Americanism was not long in coming. When it was over, the Irish had proven their loyalty without a doubt, despite a record stained by anti-draft riots that broke out in Irish neighborhoods of New York and other northern cities.

DURING THE CIVIL WAR, cities, states and even ethnic groups formed their own regiments. Many were Irish – and they wore their heritage proudly. The Irish 9th and 28th of Massachusetts both carried green flags, one with the inscription: "As aliens and strangers thou didst us befriend. As sons and true patriots we do thee defend." The Emerald Guards of the 8th Alabama Regiment wore dark green uniforms and carried a Confederate battle flag which also bore a shamrock and a harp. In 1862, William O'Meagher, a surgeon with the 29th New York, noted in his journal: "An Irish regiment with the enemy reported to have refused to fire on

ABOVE: EVEN THE Civil War could not keep Irish immigrants from coming to America when famine struck again between 1863 and 1866. The Union Army enlisted men right on the docks with food, whiskey and bounties for signing up. Top left: Irish Catholic chaplains ministered to men in combat. In 1861 the 69th New York Regiment attended Mass at their encampment in Northern Virginia. The Irish proved able leaders as well as common soldiers in the Civil War. One such commander was Colonel Mulligan (above) of Chicago.

RIGHT: CIVIL WAR regiments drew their members not only from individual states and cities but from differing national groups.

THIRD IRISH REGIMENT

From Massachusetts, and First Irish Regiment for Nine Months' Service.

25 ABLE-BODIED MEN

Wanted to fill up the Company to be commanded by

CAPTAIN WILLIAMS,

Formerly of the MASS. 24th; now of the 55TH (IRISH) MASS. REG'T.

Come with us and our IRISH HERO,

CORCORAN

Let us carry the American Eagle over the Potomac, down like an avalanche through the land of Dixie, emulating

THE GLORY of the other IRISH REGIMENTS.

$150 Bounty

And all who Enlist will receive the STATE AID.

All Recruits to this Regiment, on signing the Muster Roll, will go at once into comfortable quarters, and receive full rations of the best the market affords. Apply immediately to

Captain WILLIAMS. or. Lieut. LEONARD !

No. 109 CAMBRIDGE STREET, BOSTON.

Herald Job Office, No. 4 Williams Court, Boston.

FRANK LESLIE'S ILLUSTRATED NEWSPAPER

Entered according to the Act of Congress in the year 1856, by FRANK LESLIE, in the Clerk's Office of the District Court for the Southern District of New York.

NEW YORK, APRIL 6, 1867.

No. 601—Vol. XXIV.]

[PRICE 10 CENTS. $4 00 YEARLY. 13 WEEKS $1 00.

Belligerent Rights to the Irish Republic.

OF course these must be granted at once by the United States. There is no reasonable (Irish) mind can doubt for a moment the justice and expediency of such action. The statements made last week to President Johnson by a deputation of leading Fenians must dispel any skepticism that might linger in the mind of mere newspaper readers as to the existence of the republic. It is scarcely fair to suppose these persons capable of a deliberate falsehood, and when in reply to a question from the President, they answered that there was a *de facto* Irish Republic, we are bound, as Mr. Johnson apparently did, to believe them, and to think, with him, that it is a very serious matter; very serious for England, very serious for Ireland, and very serious for ourselves.

The conduct of Great Britain toward us during the first few months of the rebellion can never be forgotten, and, perhaps, never forgiven, at least, by this generation. Her granting belligerent rights to the rebels gave

them a standing of respectability they could never otherwise have attained. It was not diplomatically a recognition, but at least it was an acknowledgment of the existence of a power which had certain rights antagonistic to us; and while we maintained that the seceding States had no such rights, Great Britain said that they had, and took care that they were enabled to exercise them to our disadvantage. All this is an old story and perfectly familiar to our readers. Our only reason for recalling it is, that the Fenians now ask us to apply to Great Britain in their case the same principles she applied to the South when it rebelled, and if the two cases are precisely parallel there might be no good reason for denying their request. But when, on examination, we find that their case is much stronger than that of the South was, it will be impossible to refuse the small boon they ask of their adopted country.

Let us compare the two classes of aspirants for independence, and we shall see how much more worthy that of the Irish is of our recognition than the South was of that of Great Britain. In the first place, look at the length of time an

alleged oppression has been endured. Supposing the South to have suffered any wrongs from the North, which we deny, they could not have begun before the Union was formed; and what are eighty years of, at the worst, a state of unfriendliness, to the eight hundred years of sacking, and burning, and devastation, which (the Fenians tell us) their unfortunate country has borne from Great Britain?

Again, before the South was put on the footing of a nodding acquaintance with England, it had called together its own Congress, elected its own President, coined or stamped its own money, adopted a flag, raised armies, refused the process of the United States Courts within its territories, and done all that a sovereign power might or could. Have not the rebel Irish done all this and more? For instead of one President they have two, each with his own Congress or Centre—surely a double claim to eminence! They have a flag: who has not seen it? and paper money, too, and armies, and declarations of independence by the dozen. What more is wanting to a *de facto* (Irish) Republic? If it be objected that all these

fine revolutionary implements are not in Ireland, where they should be, but in the United States, the answer is obvious—that they are here merely in a state of preparation, as the rams were in Laird's shipyards, and the moment that belligerent rights are granted they will be moved to the scene of action. It may be said that granting to people within our territory belligerent rights against a friendly power is very much like going to war ourselves; and the answer is, that none but an enemy of old Ireland could make such an assertion; that the difference is quite clear to every cultivated (Irish) mind, and only a dull Saxon could fail to see it.

Besides, we have no right to assume that rebellion with all its terrors is not in full force in Ireland itself. It is not to be supposed that England, having control of the cable, would allow any message to be sent which would indicate how deadly her peril was. While as to dispatches by steamers, the two Presidents—one active, the other passive, like the Tycoon and the Mikado of the Japanese—are statesmen of too much wisdom and experience to allow any facts to leak out which should

THE RIOT ON ST. PATRICK'S DAY.—THE ATTACK ON THE POLICE AT THE CORNER OF GRAND AND PITT STREETS, NEW YORK CITY.—SEE PAGE 35.

LEFT: GREAT BRITAIN'S support of the secessionist Southern states during the early part of the Civil War was used against that power as an argument for recognition of the Irish republican cause. In supporting the granting of "Belligerent Rights" to the Irish however, Frank Leslie's Illustrated Newspaper urged that fighting be done on Irish soil rather than on the streets of New York as in the 1867 St. Patrick's Day Riot.

another carrying a green flag with our troops." However, when New York's Irish Brigade, (known as the "Fighting Irish"), made up of the 63rd, 88th and 69th New York Regiments, charged the stone wall at Marye's Heights, wearing green twigs in their hats, bellowing "Erin go bragh!" and carrying their green flags, they were shot down within twenty-five paces of their goal by the Irish 24th Georgia. In all, some 144,000 Irishmen fought for the Union, a smaller number for the Confederacy. Many gave their lives for their new country. Chicago's Irish Legion was reduced from 980 to 221. Irish Catholic chaplains and Irish nuns comforted and ministered to troops on both sides.

OBSERVED IN AMERICA as early as 1737, St. Patrick's Day has long been a major holiday in cities with large Irish populations. An engraving from the 1870s shows New York Mayor Wickham reviewing the parade at City Hall.

NOT ALL THE IRISH, however, were ready to lay down their lives for a cause they feared could work against them. Most feared that abolition of slavery would create unfair competition for the laboring jobs that many of the Irish held. And when a draft act that favored the wealthy over the poor was enacted, the Irish rebelled. In Pennsylvania the Molly Maguires stopped a train carrying draftees and offered protection to men who chose not to fight. In Boston Irish priests campaigned against

LEFT: THOUGH IT peaked in the mid-19th century, discrimination against the Irish took years to die out entirely. The rebirth of the Ku Klux Klan in 1915, added anti-Catholic to its anti-black sentiment. In this cartoon from Life *magazine, hooded Klansmen stare down the Irish and blacks in Atlanta on St. Patrick's Day.*

RIGHT: "IT SEEMS there were two Irishmen..." says Life *magazine in 1926, drawing on the belief that the Irish are always ready for a fight, for its Saint Patrick's Day issue.*

the draft – one parish meeting ended with cheers for Confederate President Jefferson Davis. Resistance, sometimes violent, occurred in Rutland, Vermont; Troy, New York; Dubuque, Iowa, and Milwaukee, Wisconsin. In New York City in July 1863, Irish rioted for three days, burning a black orphanage and the draft office, raiding houses, attacking police and killing blacks and Chinese, who apparently were dark skinned enough to be considered the enemy too. Among the police who put down the disturbance were many Irish, however. Their work earned the police the title "The Finest," an appellation still used today.

CHAPTER SIX

The Irish in the Public Eye

BY THE 1870S, THE Irish were undisputedly American. A generation had passed since the Great Famine across the sea. And the Irish were moving up from the backbreaking laboring positions they had been forced to take on their arrival. They were established. They now could capture the great prize of the American democracy: political power.

MOST NOTABLY, IN THE decade following the Civil War the Irish captured control of Tammany Hall, the New York City political machine. Founded in 1789, the Society of Tammany had, since the early 1800s, relied on and, indeed, manipulated the votes of immigrants to keep its machine in power. William Marcy Tweed – "Boss Tweed" as he later came to be known – the son of Irish immigrants, gained control of Tammany during the Civil War and, by 1870, had used its system of political spoils to enrich himself and build a huge base of power and patronage. In 1871 he was replaced by "Honest John" Kelly, another son of Irish immigrants, who, after his death in 1885, was succeeded by Richard Croker, who had emigrated from County Cork as a boy during the potato famine. Croker was succeeded by yet another Irish political boss, Charles Murphy, a former saloon keeper who ruled Tammany until his death in 1924.

THANKS TO YEARS OF political struggle against the English at home, the Irish had arrived in America with a keen interest in, and aptitude for, politics. The fact that they arrived already speaking English only made their entry into politics easier. En masse, they joined the Democratic party, which had long been closely allied with the causes of the working man. That loyalty persisted into the twentieth century. Jewish writer Harry Golden recalled that when his father was sworn in as an American citizen in 1910, the Irish judge added, in a lowered voice, "And don't forget to vote the straight Democratic ticket."

MANY IRISH, HOWEVER, HAD a passion that was divided between love of their new country, love of the old and hatred of England. Since the earliest days, the Irish in America had seen themselves as political as well as economic exiles from their

LEFT: THE IRISH in America remained politically involved in their native country from the beginning. In the 1870s, the American Clan na Gael used its "Skirmishing Fund" to support terrorist bombings in England, although most Americans advocated a non-violent solution, as suggested in this illustration of Fenian O'Donovan Rossa being "fired from the feast." Above: William Marcy "Boss" Tweed ruled New York's Tammany Hall political machine in the 1860s. In 1871, he was convicted of 104 counts of fraud and other crimes. Nast's cartoon shows the Irish closing their eyes to Tammany corruption.

native land. In the 1830s and 1840s, Irish nationalists in America gave both political and financial support to efforts to win rights for Catholics in Ireland and repeal the 1801 act that abolished the Irish Parliament. Occasionally, there were more serious anti-British incidents. In 1860, Colonel Michael Corcoran of the 69th New York Regiment refused to parade his troops for the visiting Prince of Wales – and was court martialed for the act.

RIGHT: IN 1919, Catholic clergy were among the speakers advocating freedom for Ireland at the Irish Race Convention in Philadelphia. Left: in 1972, members of the Boston Chapter of the Irish Northern Aid Committee gathered outside the British Consulate carrying crosses for 13 civilians killed by British troops in Londonderry.

BUT WITH THE FENIAN movement, founded in 1857, the nationalist movement in America took a still more serious turn. The Fenians advocated armed revolution – and counted on Irish-Americans' Ciyil War experience to achieve it. By the end of the war, the Fenians had nearly 50,000 members; in 1866, they received nearly a half million dollars in contributions. The U.S. Government even sold the Fenians guns and ammunition as part of a campaign to intimidate the British into paying war reparations for aiding the Confederacy. Then, in 1866, a force of 7,000 Fenian soldiers invaded Canada. They won their initial skirmish but later lost a legal battle with the U.S. Government, which confiscated their weapons, arrested their leaders and made it clear that an Irish nationalist army in exile would no longer be tolerated in the United States.

BUT THE IRISH DIDN'T give up their dream. The Clan na Gael, founded in 1867 as a more secretive – and more violent – nationalist group turned, from supporting political organizing and mobilizing tenant farmers, to terrorism – including a three-year bombing campaign in London in the 1880s. One conspirator, a Brooklyn

LEFT: ELIZABETH GURLEY FLYNN, who helped organize the Industrial Workers of the World, spoke to a meeting of the union in New York in 1914. A defender of the innocence of Sacco and Vanzetti and Joe Hill (she visited President Roosevelt on Hill's behalf), and an officer in the American Communist Party even into the McCarthy era, Flynn was long active in radical labor and political causes. Above: labor leader and radical leftist Tom Mooney was convicted and given a life sentence following the 1916 bombing of a Preparedness Parade in San Francisco, despite his assertion that he had been framed. For years a labor "cause," Mooney was released in 1955.

physician named Dr. Thomas Gallaher, was arrested in Birmingham, England, with enough nitroglycerin, according to contemporary accounts, to destroy all London. Gallaher received a life sentence. William Mackey Lomasney and two others were not so fortunate; they blew themselves up when a bomb they were planting under London Bridge detonated early.

MOST IRISH-AMERICANS, HOWEVER, were in favor of a peaceful solution to the problems in their homeland. Charles Stewart Parnell's parliamentary campaign in the 1870s was supported almost entirely by American money, as was that of his successor, John Redmond. The radical element did not disappear, however. One Irish organizer who toured America and visited with former Fenians and Clan na Gael members in 1914 reported wistfully, "There were no such men in Ireland." Some Irish favored Germany over Britain in World War I and many denounced President Woodrow Wilson's reluctance to bring up the Irish question with the League of Nations. But, taken as a whole, the Irish remained staunchly Democratic and staunchly American. Just as they always had, the rank and file Irish overwhelmingly voted Democratic in the 1916 election. And most Irish supported the allies in World War I. The "Fighting Irish" of the 69th New York Regiment were among the first American units sent to France.

WITH THE END OF hostilities in Ireland and the partitioning of the country in 1921, Irish American support for revolutionary causes rapidly evaporated. It lay dormant until conflict flared again in Northern Ireland in the late 1960s. Though America was said to be the main source of weapons and support for the Irish Republican Army, most Irish-Americans remained aloof. Their ancestors' homeland was by then a foreign country to them.

THE IRONY WAS THAT while the Irish generally practiced politics of passion when it came to Ireland, they practiced politics of pragmatism in their new American home, because, to the Irish, politics was a profession like any other. If their political activities provided public services, it was largely to keep voters happy and politicians in office. The result was "machine politics."

FOR AN IMMIGRANT GROUP that arrived in America destitute, the machine offered an invaluable transition to American life, providing the social services not available elsewhere. The neighborhood precinct captain brought coal in winter, beer in summer, food when the cupboard was bare and legal aid to those in trouble. The same captain, or party operatives further up the political ladder might even be able to provide the most valuable service: a government-patronage job. In Chicago, for example, forty-three percent of the policemen, firemen and watchmen in the city were first- or second-generation Irish by 1900 – though only fourteen percent of the male workforce was Irish.

SUCH A SYSTEM WAS naturally ripe for abuse. In Chicago, politicians became famous for "boodling" – the practice of selling city franchises to businesses. Vote

BELOW RIGHT: AL SMITH, "The Happy Warrior," who grew up on Manhattan's Lower East Side, apprenticed in Tammany Hall and became both mayor of New York City and governor of the state, was denied his bid for the presidency in 1928 largely as a result of anti-Catholic campaigns by the Ku Klux Klan and other organizations.

ABOVE: JOHN GOFF, one-time Supreme Court justice and in 1919 Grand Marshal of the St. Patrick's Day Parade.

FOR PRESIDENT ALFRED E. SMITH

fraud and coercion by street gangs were rampant. The system lent itself to the rise of flamboyant characters able to woo ethnic voters. New York's mayor Oakley Hall, a prime example of this, decked himself out for Saint Patrick's day 1870 with a shamrock in his lapel, green tie, green kid gloves and green coat. Moreover, the system cultivated strong ethnic power bases. For example, in 1879 twenty-seven percent of San Francisco's 38,000 voters had been born in Ireland, and the Irish ran city politics there from the time of the Civil War to the early twentieth century. As for the East Coast, during the late 1880s the Irish controlled sixty-eight cities and towns in Massachusetts.

THEN THERE WERE THE bosses. Philadelphia's Irish boss, William McMullen, was a man whose background was solidly working class. He got his start in politics with the rowdy firefighters of the Moyamensing Hose Company, and he ran a saloon for

a living. He held political office of one sort or another from 1856 until 1901. By contrast, the Fitzgeralds and the Kennedys of Boston, beginning with Mayor John F. "Honey Fitz" Fitzgerald and culminating with his grandson, President John Fitzgerald Kennedy, became as near in public perception to a royal family as America has known.

SOME OF THE BOSSES, such as Daniel Peter O'Connell – boss of Albany, New York, from 1921 until his death in 1977 – ran their dynasties from behind the scenes. A few, like Boston's flamboyant James Curley, whose political career ran from 1899 until 1949 and included four terms as mayor and four in Congress, were independent of the machine. But others made no apologies. "Of course workers get the jobs," said Jersey City boss Frank Hague about the patronage system, "What

ABOVE: IN 1914 Joseph Kennedy married Rose Fitzgerald, daughter of John F. "Honey Fitz" Fitzgerald, a colorful politician who served in the state senate, the U.S. House of Representatives and was mayor of Boston. In 1934, a Kennedy family portrait (left) included (front row) Patricia, Mr. and Mrs. Kennedy with baby Edward, Kathleen, Eunice and Rosemary as well as (back row) John, Jean and Robert. Eldest son Joseph P. Kennedy, Jr., who later was killed in World War II, was absent for the photo.

would you think of an executive who hired fellows that knocked the company or didn't take any interest in it?" Said Kansas City boss Tom Pendergast: "I'm not bragging when I say I run the show in Kansas City. I am boss. If I was a Republican they would call me 'leader.'"

THE PERSONIFICATION OF THE American political boss, however, was Richard J. Daley of Chicago. Daley lived his entire life in the working-class Irish neighborhood he was born into, but he climbed the political ladder through State House and Senate, through government and county jobs to the mayoralty of Chicago. The Irish

RIGHT: AS A young senator, John Kennedy married Jacqueline "Jackie" Lee Bouvier, the daughter of a wealthy Wall Street broker. In this 1953 news photo, the engaged couple are about to leave for a weekend of sailing at the family's Hyannis Port, Massachusetts, home. Below: when inaugurated, the 43-year-old Kennedy was the youngest man ever elected president. Kennedy, in fact, may have been more important as the first Catholic president than as an Irish president. Left: in 1960, just after John Kennedy was elected, the Kennedy clan had grown considerably, with the addition of spouses, some of whom, such as actor Peter Lawford, (far right) were as well known as the Kennedys themselves.

were still a force to be reckoned with then. When Daley first became mayor in 1955 only about ten percent of the city was Irish – yet they accounted for thirty-three percent of the city aldermen. But in an era where political machines were dying out in most cities, Daley was his own force. Head of the Democratic Party as well as mayor, he wielded enormous power (controlling as many as 30,000 patronage jobs) and, despite corruption within the machine and criticism of insensitivity to issues concerning the black community, he built a reputation for Chicago as "the city that worked." As Chicago's sixth Irish Catholic Mayor, Daley remained in power more than twenty-one years.

DALEY WAS UNIQUE. BUT his slogan, "Good government is good politics," described the attitudes of Irish politicians in any American city.

CHAPTER SEVEN

The Irish at Home and at Worship

THOUGH THEY HAD been a rural people at home, most Irish settled in cities in America, becoming the first ethnic group to live in an urban "ghetto." By 1900, some 75 percent of the Irish had crowded into seven industrial northern states, filling neighborhoods like this one in New York City to overflowing.

L IFE IN THE CITY, one of the major forces that shaped the political and public lives of the Irish, also shaped Irish family life. Bridging – and thriving in – both worlds was the Catholic Church.

WHETHER FIRST ARRIVING IN America or migrating to a new city within their new country, most Irish settled into ethnic neighborhoods. In Milwaukee in 1850, for example, forty-seven percent of the Irish lived in a single ward. Most were poor, and though they could sometimes approximate the rural housing they had known at home, most had to settle for a very different kind of urban existence. Mayor Daley's neighborhood, Bridgeport, was first called the Cabbage Patch because residents grew cabbages on vacant land. In New York, however, the density of Irish tenement neighborhoods nearly doubled when the Famine Irish arrived. The Irish urban experience is generally thought to be the first American instance of a pattern of immigrant settlement – the ghetto – that other ethnic groups would follow.

MORE IMPORTANT THAN NEIGHBORHOOD, and as important as Irishness itself to the settlers, however, was the family. Nearly all of the remittances that early immigrants sent home went, in fact, to pay for family members – most often siblings – to come to America. The family, however, did more than pay for passages. They provided a valuable transition to the New World. Without someone to meet them, arriving immigrants could be in for a rude shock. In 1829 a band of Irish immigrants landed on the Texas coast with no one to meet them, and at the same time an icy "norther" blew through. The immigrants huddled around fires made from driftwood until Mexican ranchers gave them food and clothing and found them temporary shelter in an abandoned mission. In cities, debarking immigrants often were met by "agents" who swindled them as they pretended to find them lodging or jobs. As a result, the Hibernian Society of New Orleans in the 1850s asked the city to place police on the docks to protect new arrivals, particularly the women. By 1897 a

survey taken of Irish women arriving in Boston found that only seventy-six of the 22,945 who arrived that year were not met by family members or friends.

BECAUSE SO MANY ARRIVED single, poor and wanting to earn money to send home, finding work was usually the first priority for Irish immigrants in America. And the nature of their work often kept apart the men, who labored in transient trades, and the women, who stayed put as domestics or millworkers. The result was fewer and later marriages than most other ethnic groups. In New York in the 1870s, for example, the marriage rate of the Irish was only one quarter the rate of the Germans.

AFTER MARRIAGE, HOWEVER, THESE same factors conspired to create a distinct Irish homelife. Like most immigrants, the Irish married within their own ethnic group whenever possible. But unlike many immigrant groups who welcomed newly arrived siblings, cousins and other relatives to live with them, the Irish usually lived

LEFT: BECAUSE SO many immigrants arrived impoverished, a number of American cities had Irish shantytowns such as this one in New York's Central Park. The Irish quickly prospered, however, giving rise to the distinction between first generation "shanty Irish" and the "lace curtain Irish" who succeeded them. Above: in 1898 the Chicago Post *wrote: "Scratch a convict or a pauper, and the chances are that you tickle the skin of an Irish Catholic." It's true that the "Fighting Irish" had a reputation for quick tempers and violence. The cities also had street gangs such as New York's Short-Tail Gang, photographed under a bridge in 1880.*

as nuclear families. Even when together, men and women were relatively independent of each other, having lived on their own for so long before marriage. What's more, the mobile and hazardous nature of the men's work left large numbers of deserted or widowed Irish women. In Boston in the 1870s, twenty-two percent of Irish families had women as their heads.

IRISH WOMEN WERE SUBJECT to unusual reverence. Prizefighter James J. Corbett lived with his mother for many years after he reached manhood and declared proudly that "for six years when I was a bank clerk, I gave my monthly salary to my mother …"

LIKE THE FAMILY, the Catholic Church was an institution that the Irish immigrants clung to; so much so that the influx of Irish arrivals in the mid-19th century made it the largest of all the nation's religious organizations. To this day, a large proportion of the Church's clergy and its hierarchy is of Irish descent. St. Patrick's Cathedral (left), New York, has served the Irish of the city since its opening in 1879, while Boston's Cathdral of the Holy Cross (right) is the mother church for that city's large Irish Catholic community. Above: Cardinal William H. O'Connell, archbishop of Boston from 1907-1944.

HOWEVER, IRISH WOMEN ALSO had to shoulder unusual responsibility. Author Eugene O'Neill, whose father abandoned the family and returned to Ireland, wrote that his mother was reduced to "slaving as a charwoman, the family always ill-fed and poorly clad." Irish women often had to fight the battles that the poor always face – hunger, illiteracy, drunkenness, crime – alone. Many families had the prop of a strong women to enable them to climb out of that poverty.

WHEREVER THERE IS DIFFICULTY, people also often look to religion for support. The Irish were no exception in their need for spiritual comfort, but the Catholic Church also provided many of the social services that were not forthcoming from

government or secular charities: hospitals, orphanages, asylums and almshouses. Prime examples of Church affiliated helpers were the Society of St. Vincent de Paul, which provided food and shelter for the poor; the Sisters of the Good Shepherd, who worked to save women from prostitution, and the Sisters of Mercy, who provided shelter and employment assistance for young women. These are just a few of the Catholic agencies that assisted the new immigrants.

THE CATHOLIC CHURCH, HOWEVER, was probably more important for its role in creating an Irish-American ethnic identity. For while Irish people had been emigrating to America for two centuries, only in the mid-nineteenth century did the words "Irish" and "Catholic" became synonymous. There are two reasons for this. First, Catholicism was one of the objects of English repression in Ireland. Such repression is certain to bind any people together. Second, and consequently, the Irish were the first large Catholic group to emigrate to America. From numbering one percent of the population in the 1790 census, the number of Catholics grew to over seven percent in 1850 and to ten percent – constituting the nation's largest single faith – in 1860. Immigration following the potato famine caused a tremendous growth in the Catholic population – from less than one million in 1840 to about three million in 1860.

RIGHT: WORKINGMEN GATHERED in 1907 for an ale and a pipe at a bar where a poster on the mirror advertised a ball at Tammany Hall. In America, the Irish continued the European tradition of tavern as men's social club. Above: in Slater's tavern, New York.

IRISH ATTENDED PAROCHIAL schools more than any other Catholic group. These schools not only taught religion, they reinforced the contributions of Irish and Catholics to history and culture – subjects generally ignored by the public schools.

WITH THE INFLUX of the Irish in the mid-19th century, and other Catholic ethnic groups later, the Catholic Church increased its role in providing social services, from hospitals, orphanages and almshouses to schools.

THE KNOW-NOTHING PARTY, anti-Catholic riots of the 1850s, and "No Irish Need Apply" notices in newspaper advertisements and shop windows were direct results of the Irish Catholic influx. As with English persecution, however, anti-Irish feeling drew the Irish-Americans closer together. In 1892, a railroad worker in Iowa described his relationship to others this way: "… snakes, squirrels, wolves, Indians, Negroes, Germans, Swedes and Norwegians, and Yankees. The community I live in is composed of all of these classes. They all hate an Irishman, but there is no love lost, an Irishman does not care much for them."

WHILE THE PRESBYTERIAN IRISH who immigrated in earlier years met with established Protestant churches, Irish Catholics were often left to their own devices – making for a need that also helped create an Irish community. The late nineteenth century, for example, saw a tremendous boom in church building, much of it in Irish neighborhoods. Between 1880 and 1900 in Chicago, for example, more English-speaking parishes were organized than in all the years since the Chicago diocese was established in 1842. From Windsor Locks, Connecticut, to Utica, New York, and westward, Irish canal and railroad workers formed Catholic parishes wherever they stopped to put down roots. Especially in places where the Irish were not welcome, the Catholic parish would serve to divide a large, hostile city into smaller, more manageable units that a newcomer could understand and become involved with.

In such a parish, the priest became not only a spiritual leader but a community leader. Between 1780 and 1935, some fifty-eight percent of the 464 Catholic bishops appointed in America were Irish. In 1970, half the American bishops and a third of the priests in the Catholic Church were Irish.

THE IRISH, AS A result, were steeped in religion from cradle to grave – especially during their school years, when many of them attended Catholic establishments. Here they received instruction not only in the Catholic faith but in such subjects as Irish history and the Catholic contribution to American history. The Irish, in fact, were the most ardent supporters of America's parochial schools. In Chicago, sixty-five percent of students enrolled in Catholic schools in 1876 were Irish. By 1917, more than eighty percent of Chicago's Catholic parishes maintained schools. Such enthusiasm was not universal, however. In Boston, twenty-five percent of public-

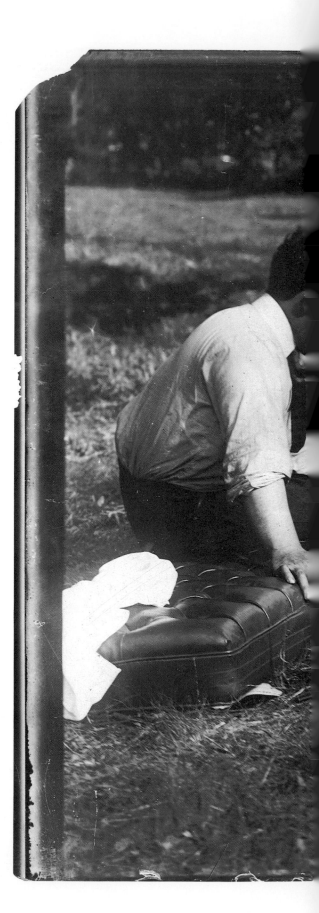

ABOVE: THE McNULTY family provides traditional entertainment. Right: weather permitting, holidays were an opportunity for a picnic, such as this one in 1915, made possible by the automobile – note the seat cushion removed for the occasion at left. Note, also, the bucket of beer from the local tavern.

school teachers were Irish Catholics by the early twentieth century, and in San Francisco, where compulsory reading of the Protestant Bible had been abolished as early as 1854, a greater number of Irish attended public schools. In such cases, some Irish parents chose public schools as an ideal way to assimilate themselves and their children into American society. Nonetheless, the children of Irish communities on average attended Catholic schools more consistently and for longer than those of German, Italian or any other ethnic groups.

WHETHER THEY CONSCIOUSLY SOUGHT to assimilate or not, education was perceived by them as the way for the Irish to attain the American dream. In Boston, public-school enrollment nearly doubled during the ten years that included the famine immigration.

EMIGRANT GROUPS ALWAYS bring their songs and dances with them, and the Irish were no exception. Those who kept the traditional music alive included the young New Jersey fiddle players in 1928 (below left), pipe player James A. Heyden (below) in the 1920s, and the New York step dancer (right) in the 30s. Today, Irish music is enjoying a renewed popularity among young folk music fans.

THE IRISH WORKED FOR their education – Irish children were more likely than the children of any other immigrants to have to hold down jobs in addition to attending school. And by the late nineteenth century, Catholic universities such as Fordham, Notre Dame, Holy Cross, and Boston College were predominantly Irish in the ethnic composition of both student body and faculty.

CHAPTER EIGHT

The Irish Today

BY THE 1890S, THE Irish had divided themselves into yet more groups. Not only were there Catholic and Protestant Irish, now there were "Lace-Curtain" and "Shanty" Irish. The social position of the "Shanty" Irish may be obvious in the appellation: they had not progressed much from the desperate poverty of their beginnings. The "Lace-Curtain" Irish, on the other hand, had progressed to owning — or aspiring to own — such luxuries as the curtains that gave them their name.

ON THE WAY UP, the Irish had overcome the negative stereotypes that had dogged them since their arrival in America. They owed part of their eventual success and assimilation to the arrival of new southern- and eastern-European ethnic groups. These newcomers were even more different and posed an even greater threat than the Irish had to the English-based American establishment. The decline in Irish immigration that occurred at the same time also helped. For it meant that by the early twentieth century most Irish in America were not newcomers at all. Instead, they were second or third generation Irish-Americans. In the Famine years, the Irish had accounted for nearly half of all immigration. But from 1900 to 1910 the Irish numbered only three percent — and by the 1960s only about one percent — of immigrants. Part of the decline in the 1960s was due to adverse changes in the immigration law. Seeking to compensate for the inequities such changes entailed, the Immigration Act of 1990 singled out the Irish for extra immigrant visas — giving them about 2.3 percent of the total. Besides, recent immigration had tended to include professionals and other highly trained persons, rather than the unskilled laborers of earlier generations.

UNTIL THE SECOND DECADE of the twentieth century, the Irish in America had suffered from their history. Poverty and political oppression at home had been a real handicap, and involvement in Irish nationalist causes had been a distraction from improving their lives in America. By the twentieth century, however, the Famine was ancient history. And with the creation of the Irish Free State, nationalism all but disappeared. At the same time, Irish-American accomplishments opened the

BORN IN ROXBURY, Massachusetts in 1858, the son of an Irish immigrant, John L. Sullivan began his boxing career when matches were still bare knuckle fights. He quickly rose to world heavyweight champion and won 200 contests, including the marathon 75-round (2 hours, 16 minutes) fight against Jack Kilrain in 1889 .

way for the success and assimilation that formed part of the American Dream.

AS EARLY AS WORLD WAR I, Irish families were already sending more of their children to college than the average American family. Their chances of achieving a managerial or white collar position were accordingly greater than the American average, too. By the 1970s, according to national statistics, Irish Catholics had overtaken Irish Protestants and British Protestants as well in terms of total years spent in education, occupational prestige and income. Only Jews were more successful as an ethnic group. Had not so many young men become priests and so many women become nuns, the Irish level of achievement in secular and material terms would have been even greater.

HISTORICALLY, THE IRISH FOUND success easier in the West, where everybody was a newcomer, than in the East, where they had to battle entrenched establishments.

ABOVE LEFT: IN 1873, John P. Holland emigrated to America, where he built the first successful submarine. His work was partially financed by the radical Fenians, who hoped to use the craft against the British Navy. In 1900, he provided the U.S. Navy with its first operational submarine, the U.S.S. Holland. Above: born in Colorado, Jack Dempsey began fighting in mining camps in 1912 and became heavyweight champion in 1919. He lost the title to Gene Tunney in 1926, ending Irish dominance of the sport.

RIGHT: HENRY FORD, whose father fled the Irish potato famine in the 1840s, pioneered the assembly line method of manufacturing to create one of the largest automobile companies in the world. In the 1920s, the Ford Motor Company opened a plant in Ireland. Below: son of an Irish dancing teacher who arrived in Boston in 1847, Louis Henri Sullivan became one of the pioneers of modern architecture. Through his practice in Chicago, he refined both the design of large metal frame commercial buildings and the theory of organic architecture. He made famous the phrase "Form follows function."

Wherever they settled, however, the Irish were firm believers in the bootstrap theory: with enough hard work anyone could escape poverty. One theory claims that poverty and lack of business skills actually aided the Irish in their business success and cultural assimilation. Forced to work for American bosses for a generation or two, the Irish learned the American way of doing business, so that when they did open their own businesses they were not hampered by Old-World ways.

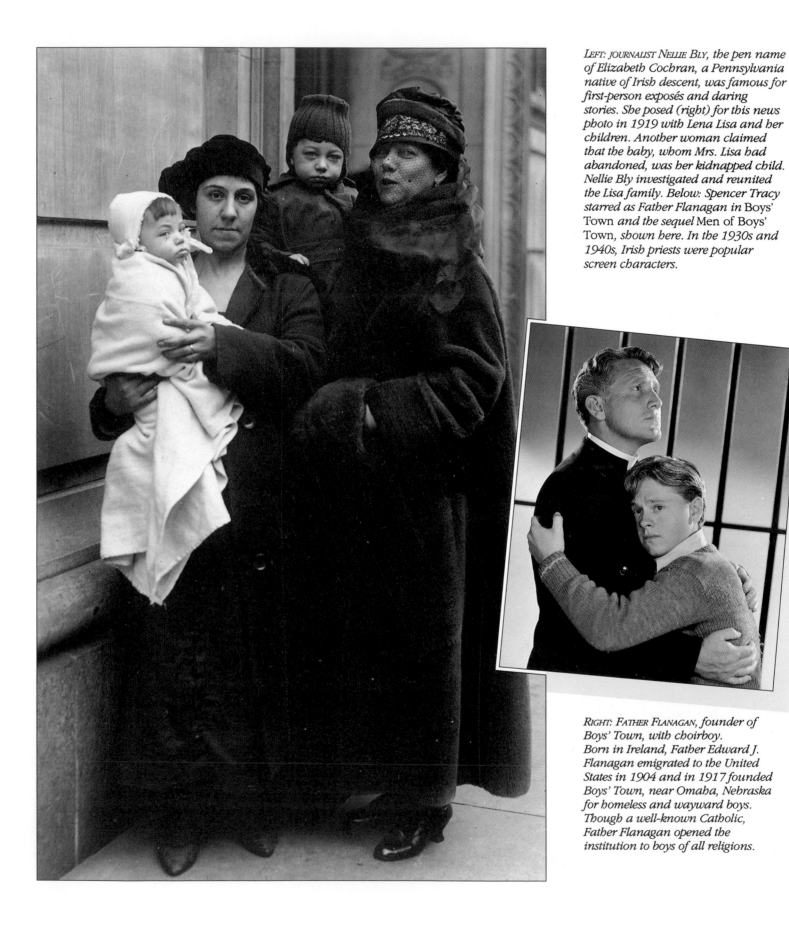

LEFT: JOURNALIST NELLIE BLY, the pen name of Elizabeth Cochran, a Pennsylvania native of Irish descent, was famous for first-person exposés and daring stories. She posed (right) for this news photo in 1919 with Lena Lisa and her children. Another woman claimed that the baby, whom Mrs. Lisa had abandoned, was her kidnapped child. Nellie Bly investigated and reunited the Lisa family. Below: Spencer Tracy starred as Father Flanagan in Boys' Town *and the sequel* Men of Boys' Town, *shown here. In the 1930s and 1940s, Irish priests were popular screen characters.*

RIGHT: FATHER FLANAGAN, founder of Boys' Town, with choirboy. Born in Ireland, Father Edward J. Flanagan emigrated to the United States in 1904 and in 1917 founded Boys' Town, near Omaha, Nebraska for homeless and wayward boys. Though a well-known Catholic, Father Flanagan opened the institution to boys of all religions.

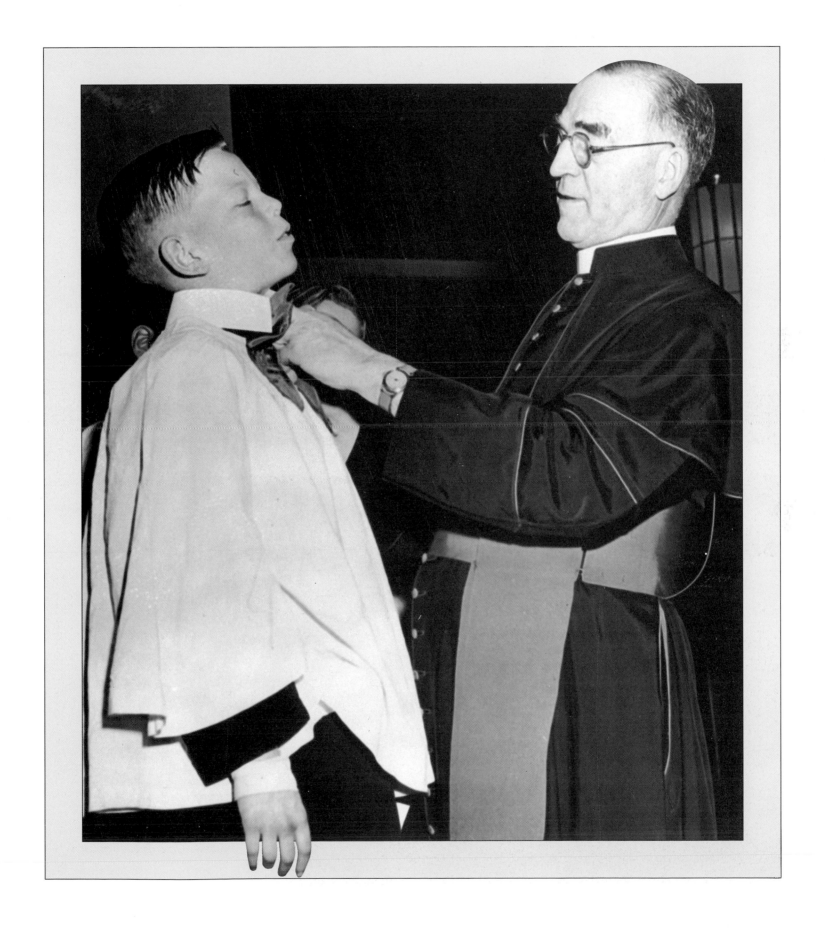

Left: in On the Waterfront, *Karl Malden played Father Barry, an Irish priest who inspired longshoremen to overthrow a corrupt labor boss. Below left: George M. Cohan expressed Irish-American patriotism well with such songs as "Yankee Doodle Dandy," "Over There," and "It's a Grand Old Flag." Right: the stage Irishman, a bumbling, belligerent, drunken buffoon, had been a stereotype of the American theater since the early 19th century. Twentieth-century actors such as Buster Keaton, who played a never smiling, wide-eyed innocent in the early days of the cinema, however, built their own style of humor from the Irish comic tradition. Far right: Father Charles Coughlin, the Depression era "Radio Priest," preyed on the fear and anxiety of the times as he cast blame for economic woes. His initial targets were bankers, government bureaucrats and the wealthy. But his growing anti-Semitism, attacks on popular figures like President Roosevelt, and other excesses, led to his downfall.*

THE AMERICAN-IRISH BELIEF in self-help occasionally brought charges of insensitivity, much like those leveled by blacks at Chicago's Mayor Daley. The Irish who remained at the bottom of the economic scale occasionally had conflicts with other racial and ethnic groups: one case was the violence that erupted in Boston in the 1970s over school integration. The fact is, however, that generally Catholic Irish were the second most liberal of all ethnic groups – again, after Jews – backing such political and social causes as integration, civil liberties and feminism.

BY THE 1920s, MANY Irish identified more closely with their religion than their homeland. The Knights of Columbus, which stressed Americanism along with Catholicism, was the fastest growing Irish-American organization in Chicago during the early twentieth century. By mid-century, more Irish identified with their parish than their homeland, and John Kennedy was more important as the nation's first Catholic president than as an Irish president. (There have, after all, been eleven Protestant-Irish presidents from Andrew Jackson to Jimmy Carter. Ronald Reagan, whose ancestors were Irish Catholics, was raised as a Presbyterian.)

TODAY, SOME FOURTEEN TO sixteen million Americans, six to seven percent of the total population, are entirely or mostly of Irish extraction – and about three times that number have a smaller proportion of Irish blood. Most live where they always have: about seventy percent live in cities in the north and west – with sixty percent of those resident in the New-England and Middle-Atlantic States. Among Irish Protestants, nearly seventy percent live in the south. True to their roots, and in contrast to the northern Catholics, many live rural lives.

ON MARCH 17, HOWEVER, Americans of all types all over the country wear green in celebration of St. Patrick's Day. In Chicago, the stripes down the middle of Dearborn Street are painted green for the St. Patrick's Day Parade – and the Chicago River is dyed green. There are green derby hats and green balloons and green windbreakers everywhere you look. Labor unions and Democratic organizations and a pipe band from the Chicago Police Department participate in the Parade. There are also marching bands from public and parochial schools, playing songs like *When Irish Eyes are Smiling*. Many of the musicians have shamrocks painted on their cheeks. But many of the musicians are black. Or Hispanic. Or from any of dozens of ethnic groups that are not Irish, perhaps because St. Patrick's Day is the one ethnic holiday that has been wholeheartedly embraced by the American public. In New York, Italian Governor Mario Cuomo, black Mayor David Dinkins and Jewish former mayor Edward Koch marched down Fifth Avenue with the St. Patrick's Day parade. Said Koch: "Only in New York do you have a St. Patrick's Day Parade with a governor, Mario Cuomo, marching with the invalids in wheelchairs, the Mayor marching with gays and lesbians, and me, a Jewish boy … marching with the police department's Holy Name Society."

RIGHT: AMERICA'S MOST decorated World War II serviceman was a Texas-Irish sharecropper's son named Audie Murphy. Recipient of 28 American and foreign medals, including the Congressional Medal of Honor, Murphy singlehandedly held off a German force of more than 200 men and half a dozen tanks. After the war, he became a Hollywood actor, starring in his own story, To Hell and Back *(1955), and other films.*

ABOVE: DAUGHTER OF John B. Kelly, a 1936 Olympic oarsman and one-time candidate for mayor of Philadelphia, Grace Kelly was the reigning movie star of the early 1950s. She retired in 1956 to marry Prince Ranier of Monaco. Left: The Quiet Man, *one of four films for which John Ford won Academy Awards as best director, starred Irish actress Maureen O'Hara with John Wayne. Despite her family roots, O'Hara had to wait 13 years for the chance to play an Irishwoman in this film.*

LEFT: PROBABLY THE *best known Southern Irish-American was Scarlett O'Hara, heroine of the film* Gone With the Wind. *Right: James Dunn won an Academy Award for his portrayal of an alcoholic Irish singing waiter in* A Tree Grows in Brooklyn. *The film from Betty Smith's novel is the sad tale of the Nolan family as they struggle to rise above poverty in turn-of-the-century New York.*

ABOVE: GENE KELLY, *an athletic dancer with a twinkle in his eye, brought a playful freshness to the screen that included dancing with cartoon characters Tom and Jerry. Right: tenement life could be played for laughs, as in the 1950s television series* The Honeymooners. *Stars Gleason and Carney updated the harebrained, flamboyant stage Irishman to loveable characters without the negative characteristics of drink and violence that had plagued the Irish for years.*

St. Patrick's Day has been assimilated just as the Irish have. But just as St. Patrick's Day still is unmistakably Irish – even with others participating – so are the Irish-Americans. Ethnic traits seldom die out entirely. Families transmit them from generation to generation. So do neighborhoods and churches, politics and the arts, the cinema and other cultural bodies. Who can deny the Irishness of John L. Sullivan or the Mighty Casey; James Cagney or Bing Crosby; Notre Dame "Fighting Irish" football or Boston Celtics basketball; Al Smith or Joseph McCarthy; Boys Town's Father Flanagan or the U.S. Senate's Tip O'Neill?.

Irish Americans, no matter how many generations removed from Ireland, are still interested in their roots and in their heritage. Chicago writer Finley Peter Dunne's character Mr. Dooley, a philosophizing Irish Chicago saloon keeper, longed for a history "that'll show me th' people fightin', gettin' dhrunk, makin' love, gettin' married, owin' th' grocery man an' bein' without hard coal." In a similar vein, the Irish want to remember the entire character of their history, not just its grand events. The late-twentieth-century interest in cultural pluralism has only helped matters and dignified a quest for cultural and ethnic identity. For the Irish, as for many Americans, their sense of ethnic history is alive and well and thriving in the present.

Members of the Emerald Society of the New York Fire Department proudly march through the streets of the city during the St. Patrick's Day Parade.

WRAPPED IN THE Stars and Stripes, these young boys take as much pride and interest in their roots during the St. Patrick's Day Parade as does the member of an earlier generation (below).